The lion's p

Story written by Gill Munton
Illustrated by Tim Archbold

Speed Sounds

Consonants

Ask children to say the sounds.

f	l	m	n	r	s	v	z	sh	th	ng
ff	ll	mm	nn	rr	ss	ve	zz			nk
ph	le	mb	kn	wr	se		se			
			(gn)		c		s			
					(ce)					

b	c	d	g	h	j	p	qu	t	w	x	y	ch
bb	k	dd	gg		g	pp		tt	wh			tch
	ck		(gu)		ge							

Each box contains one sound but sometimes more than one grapheme.
*Focus graphemes for this story are **circled**.*

Vowels

Ask children to say the sounds in and out of order.

a	e ea	i	o	u	ay a͡-e a	ee ea y e	igh i͡-e ie i	ow o͡-e o oe
at	hen	in	on	up	day	see	high	blow

oo u͡-e ue	oo	ar	**or** **oor** **ore** **aw**	air are	ir ur er	ou ow	oy oi
zoo	look	car	for	fair	whirl	shout	boy

5

Story Green Words

den paw thorn sore dawn raw straw slops jaws
sword*

Ask children to say the syllables and then read the whole word.

Ro|man cir|cus migh|ty loy|al And|ro|cles*

Ask children to read the root first and then the whole word with the suffix.

crawl → crawled   gnash → gnashing   yawn → yawned

peace → peacefully   feast → feasting   gnaw → gnawing

scorn → scornfully   jeer → jeering

* Challenge Words

6

Vocabulary Check

Discuss the meaning (as used in the story) after the children have read each word.

	definition:	**sentence:**
den	*a cave where animals live*	*The cave was a lion's den!*
mighty	*large and powerful*	*The lion opened his mighty jaws.*
thorn	*sharp twig*	*A sharp thorn was stuck deep …*
paw	*animal's foot*	*… in the lion's paw.*
scornfully	*nastily*	*"You have broken the law," he shouted scornfully.*
slops	*horrid, watery soup*	*He had straw to sleep on and slops to eat.*
jeering	*shouting and teasing*	*There were thousands of people shouting and jeering.*

Red Words

Ask children to practise reading the words across the rows, down the columns and in and out of order clearly and quickly.

many	could	one	are
were	other	through	was
call	to	there	they
said	all	does	want
what	come	any	should

The lion's paw

This is a story about a Roman slave called Androcles.
His master treated him so badly that, one day,
he ran away.

Androcles needed a place to sleep.
So when he saw a cave,
dug out of the hillside,
he crawled inside.

As Androcles lay resting, he saw
a pile of bones on the floor.
Then he saw a long, golden hair. A lion's hair!
The cave was a lion's den!

Before he could run away,
a shadow fell across the floor.
The lion was back!

The lion opened his mighty jaws,
Gnashing his teeth and flashing
his claws,
And then he stretched out on the
dusty floor.
Looked up at Androcles, held out
his paw …

"Poor beast," said Androcles.
For a sharp thorn was stuck deep in the lion's paw.
He took the sore paw in his hands, and pulled the thorn until it
came out. The lion yawned, and was soon snoring peacefully.

The lion woke at dawn and went hunting.
Soon, Androcles was feasting on fresh, raw meat,
and the lion was gnawing the bones.

Androcles and the lion lived happily in the cave for many months.

But Androcles was a man, not a lion,
and he needed to be with other men.
He shook the lion by the paw,
and set off back to Rome.

But his wicked master saw him.
"You have broken the law,"
he shouted scornfully,
"and you must be punished!"

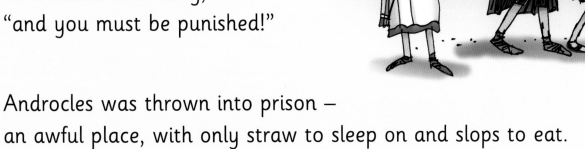

Androcles was thrown into prison –
an awful place, with only straw to sleep on and slops to eat.

The next morning, the guard spoke to Androcles.
"You are going to be thrown to the lions," he said.

Androcles was given a sword and a helmet,
and pushed through a huge wooden door.
He found himself in a sort of circus ring,
with thousands of people shouting and jeering.

Then, across the ring,
he saw the lion – huge, growling and
angry.

A strange thing happened next.

The lion opened his mighty jaws,
Gnashing his teeth, and flashing his claws,
And then he stretched out on the dusty floor,
Looked up at Androcles, held out his paw.

It was the lion from the cave!

Androcles took the paw, and kissed it. There were loud cheers from the people. They had never seen a man kissing a lion's paw before! They began to chant: "Set them free! Set them free!"

Androcles and the loyal lion were freed, and lived together for ever more.

Questions to talk about

Ask children to TTYP each question using 'Fastest finger' (FF) or 'Have a think' (HaT).

p.9   (FF)   Why did Androcles run away?

p.10   (FF)   How did Androcles know the lion was back?

p.11   (HaT)   How could Androcles tell that the lion wasn't going to hurt him?

p.12   (FF)   What did Androcles eat when he was living with the lion?

p.13   (HaT)   Why had Androcles broken the law?

p.14   (HaT)   What do you think the crowds were there to see?

p.15   (HaT)   Why did the crowds shout "Set them free!"?

Questions to read and answer

(Children complete without your help.)

1. Where did Androcles go when he ran away?

2. How did Androcles help the lion?

3. Why was Androcles thrown in prison?

4. What did Androcles expect the lion to do?

5. Why did the people want to set Androcles and the lion free?

Speedy Green Words

saw	inside	pile	shadow
month	awful	angry	strange
place	before	story	sleep
about	across	happily	next
teeth	took	found	awful